PADDLE STEAMERS
OF THE THAMES

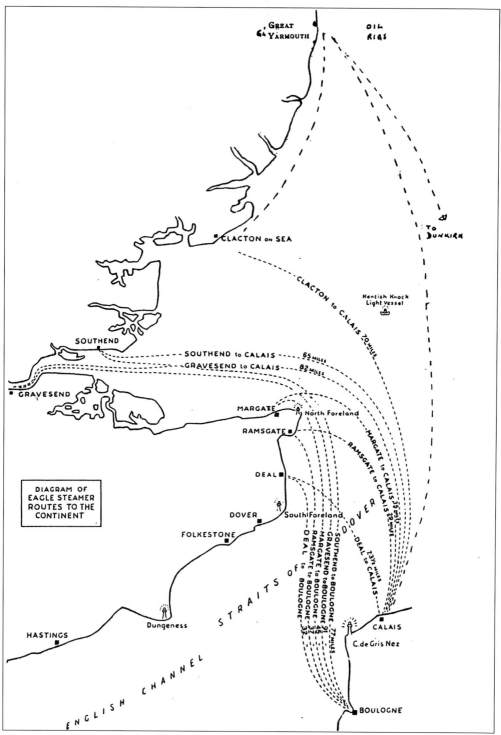

This map of the Thames Estuary was published by the General Steam Navigation Company, c.1959.

PADDLE STEAMERS
OF THE THAMES

Peter Box

TEMPUS

First published 2000
Reprinted 2000, 2004

Tempus Publishing Limited
The Mill, Brimscombe Port,
Stroud, Gloucestershire, GL5 2QG
www.tempus-publishing.com

British Library Cataloguing in Publication Data.
A catalogue record for this book is available from the British Library.

ISBN 0 7524 1731 2

Typesetting and origination by Tempus Publishing Limited.
Printed in Great Britain.

The *Golden Eagle*, built in 1909 and seen here c.1935, was probably of the most famous and most fondly remembered of the Thames paddle steamers. She was a feature of summer holidays to Kent for over forty years and was to serve her country in two world wars.

Contents

More normally associated with Lulworth Cove, Dorset, than the Thames, the beautiful Victorian paddle steamer *Consul* is seen here leaving Southend Pier, during September 1963. Chartered to New Belle Steamers Ltd, the *Consul*'s Thames 'career' lasted for just one week.

Notes on the Photographs

The first illustrations of Thames paddle steamers appear in paintings of the 1820s and 1830s. Periodiacals occasionally recorded the arrivals of new vessels, but seldom with a drawing. It is a fact that we do not know with certainty what some of the early Thames vessels looked like. In the 1860s there was a surge in development with the arrival of more 'modern' vessels originating from the Clyde. Some of these steamers were depicted in drawings that reflect a degree of artistic licence. The first photographic records tend to be found in the 1870s, but these views are very rare. After 1890, photographs of Thames paddle steamers become more common, but good views are not found as frequently as those of paddle steamers in other areas of Great Britain. The photographs included within these pages reflect this imbalance, in the same way as they reflect the social fashions of the times depicted.

Dating early photographs with accuracy is difficult. One has to rely on the accuracy of others or one's own detective work. Within these captions I have attempted to be as accurate as possible. The 'Belle Steamers' are referred to frequently within the text. This company had many different titles over the years, and so, for clarity, I have deliberately referred to them by their colloquial name, 'Belle Steamers'. Further details on this company's nomenclature can be found in the book, *Belles of the East Coast*.

Introduction

The history of Thames paddle steamers – steamers that transported millions of holidaymakers to and from the riverside and coastal resorts – can be traced long before the advent of photography. Their popularity, as a means of transport along the river, began in the 1820s and developed, with the help of technology, in the decades that followed. Originally, the Thames paddle steamer services were all year round, with passengers sharing deck space with other cargoes, even livestock. There are numerous accounts of people experiencing harrowing night journeys to Great Yarmouth during the winter months, sleeping on deck with only a blanket for comfort. Some vessels had a few berths for passengers, but accounts suggest that drunkenness and sickness often made such accommodation uninhabitable. During the 1840s these mixed cargo and passenger vessels began to be supplemented by more modern, 'passenger-only' steamers, on the popular routes to Kent. Often these new vessels appeared only in the summer months, and the term 'butterfly boats' has been used to describe them. However, these changes took time and it wasn't until 1868 that the General Steam Navigation Company's paddle steamer *Albion*, made the first daytime 'passenger-only' journey to the established resort of Great Yarmouth.

By the time of the 1871 Bank Holidays Act, steamer routes were well established. The Thames was the arterial highway of the Empire and London its focal point. Soon the 'day trip' and the 'long weekend' became a necessity, a requirement for those working in the city and its suburbs. In the days before the completion of the railway network and certainly before motor buses, the paddle steamers offered a means of escape from the daily drudgery of work, to the 'glamorous' resorts of Kent, Essex and East Anglia. However, it would be wrong to think of these paddle steamers as just excursion vessels; for many, particularly in the years before 1914, they were the principal way of getting to a holiday destination. With their origins and subsequent development, deeply rooted in these essential services, the Thames paddle steamers may have differed from some of those found elsewhere in the British Isles. As Victoria's reign developed, so did technology and the demands of people. By the time the Edwardian decade commenced, the Thames paddle steamers' routes ranged from Dover to Great Yarmouth and across the Channel to the sophisticated resorts of Belgium and France. The ships and their operators helped establish towns, piers – often built solely for their use – and the popularity of beaches. They effectively changed forever the landscape of the Thames coast.

Unlike some other areas of Britain, no one company dominated Thames routes. Instead, a large number of separate companies developed, prospered and eventually succumbed to competition or changing times, only to be replaced by others. This has given the researcher variety, but also difficulties as, in many cases, company records either do not exist or are frustratingly incomplete. Only the General Steam Navigation Company was there at the beginning and at the end of paddle steamer operations on the Thames.

Until the First World War the paddle steamers were well able to compete with other forms of transport. Indeed, economic prosperity and fashions meant that there were enough passengers for all. On an Edwardian Bank Holiday it was not unusual for four paddle steamers to make the long journey to Great Yarmouth, while a similar number could be seen at Southend, Margate and Ramsgate. Those hardy 'excursionists' – usually referred to as 'freight' by the contemporary press – were not wealthy merchants or the privileged few; they were the factory workers, shopkeepers and salesmen of the day: the hardworking artisans on whom Victorian prosperity was built. The excursions on which they embarked were not cheap, not something to be decided upon a whim. They were planned and saved for over the year. Their departure was an exciting time, the vessels being waved away from their Thames-side piers by hundreds of onlookers. On arrival at a resort, passengers – however tired or ill – were met by others. This time it was the local lodging-house keepers and hoteliers touting for business. Their numbers could reach over a thousand and often required a police presence to maintain order and public safety. Resorts could be so busy that some passengers, left without accommodation, would wander the streets, sleep on the beaches or even try to re-board the steamers in search of a berth for the night.

The events of the summer of 1914 changed the face of Britain and, in so doing, changed a way of life. The paddle steamers were not immune from this and, although many vessels returned in 1919, their clientele had changed. Passengers were more demanding and 'forward looking', keen to exploit the new technology that the war had brought about. They were not content to return to the old order.

The Thames coast resorts maintained their popularity with 'excursionists', but the means of arrival reflected a demand for speed and a reduced journey time. The numbers of paddle steamers fell, as many of the older vessels found their way to the scrapyards. The new tonnage reflected the new age: the new vessels were large, fast, sleek and equipped with the latest machinery. Out went coal and in came oil. By the mid-1930s the very concept of a paddle steamer was being threatened by the new propeller-driven, diesel-powered vessels that were starting to appear. Fast, luxuriously appointed and, at the height of the depression, economically efficient, these motor vessels could be started at the touch of a button and needed far fewer crew. I make no apology for including within this book some of those vessels, as they played an important part in the story of Thames paddle steamers. With such vessels in mind, it could be argued that the Second World War only delayed the final demise of the traditional Thames 'paddler'.

By the late 1950s only one, *Medway Queen*, remained. This 'heroine' of Dunkirk soldiered on, to the delight of thousands, until she too succumbed to economic pressure after the end of the 1963 season, and moved on to fulfil a new static role on the Isle of Wight. Her departure brought to an end over 140 continuous years of Thames paddle steamer excursions.

The decline in the number of Thames paddle steamers was mirrored in other parts of the United Kingdom. Today, nostalgia is a powerful force: it is financially lucrative and attracts business. In the late 1960s and early 1970s this was not the case. The remaining paddle steamers were removed, often unceremoniously, from the South Coast, Bristol Channel and Scotland, to the scrapyards. With those vessels died – often literally – a Victorian heritage. By 1966 the large Thames motor vessels, that had in part been responsible for the demise of the paddle steamers, had themselves passed into history.

Today, only one seagoing paddle steamer remains in operation – the *Waverley*. In 1974 this vessel was sold to the Paddle Steamer Preservation Society for £1, with the challenge to maintain her. It is *Waverley*'s yearly visits to the Thames and the coastal resorts of Kent and Essex that allow us to recapture part of what we have lost. The Thames is also graced by the small river paddle steamer *Kingswear Castle* which has been beautifully restored and can usually be seen on the river Medway. In recent years, those wishing to experience the long East Coast journey from London to Great Yarmouth, have been fortunate to have the restored motor vessel *Balmoral* visit the Thames and revive that exhilarating excursion.

Of all the traditional Thames paddle steamers, only *Medway Queen* remains. She has now returned to the Medway and her survival is the key objective of the Medway Queen Preservation Society. However, although their efforts are clearly visible on her frail structure, her future is by no means assured.

Those who have travelled on paddle steamers will never forget the noise, smell and vibrations of that particular form of transport. During a trip there was always time to reflect on life, converse with friends and enjoy the sights that passed. You travelled at a slow speed, a leisurely speed that today we haven't time for.

One
The Formative Years:
1865-1900

THE SALOON STEAM-PACKET COMPANY'S VESSEL ALEXANDRA, FOR PASSENGER TRAFFIC ON THE THAMES,

Probably the most influential of all the Thames paddle steamers was the Saloon Steam Packet Company's *Alexandra*. This view dates from 1865 when she appeared on the river for the first time. From the start, she set a standard of luxury that all other paddle steamer operators had to emulate if they were to survive and remain in competition. Sadly, this fine vessel was wrecked at London Bridge in September 1889.

In September 1878, the London Steamboat Company's steamer *Princess Alice* sank after colliding with the collier *Bywell Castle,* near the Becton Gasworks. She was returning from Gravesend with a full complement of passengers and it has been estimated that as many as 700 people were drowned. This view, from a contemporary *London Illustrated News,* reflects the horror that the passengers must have experienced at the moment of impact.

The *Princess Alice* had been built for Clyde services as the *Bute.* She was perhaps lucky to survive the storms that battered both she and her sister vessel, *Kyles,* on their delivery voyage to the Thames in the winter of 1866. Although always structurally suspect, *Princess Alice* was a firm favourite with the London public and had transported the Shah of Persia during his visit to London in 1873.

The remains of the *Princess Alice* after they had been dragged from the river. So many died that temporary mortuaries needed to be set up throughout the disaster area. Even the London Steamboat Company's chairman lost his wife and child in the tragedy.

Thames Steamboat Collision Relief Fund.

No. __10__   Town Hall, Brighton, *14th octor* 1878.

Received of *S. Reeves Smith Esq*

the sum of *One* pounds *eight* shillings and *five* pence,

being Subscription to the above Fund. — *the amount deposited in a collection box at the Brighton aquarium*

£ 1 : 8 : 5   *Fred Dunkley*

For the Honorary Secretary.

The nation was so shocked by this disaster that a 'Relief Fund' was quickly established. This receipt is for money collected at the Brighton Aquarium.

One of the best known of the early saloon steamers on the Thames was the *Glen Rosa*. Built in 1877, she appeared on the Thames in 1881 and was originally owned by the London Steamboat Company. She was a popular vessel and, although not always mechanically reliable, was used on a range of services from Great Yarmouth to Ramsgate and across the Channel. She is seen here at the opening of the new Ipswich Lock in 1881, her first Thames season.

The *Glen Rosa* was used on a service between Great Yarmouth and Harwich in the summer of 1893. Under the command of Captain Reader, this proved to be a popular service, although breakdowns appear to have been frequent. It was probably the *Glen Rosa*'s speed and size that resulted in her being moved to Kent in 1894.

Typical of the older, smaller Thames paddle steamers was the *Lady of Lorne*. Built in 1871, this vessel was owned by the Medway Steam Packet Company. She is seen here while leaving Southend Pier, probably for the Medway towns. The date of the photograph is unknown, but the vessel was scrapped during 1899.

The Medway Steam Packet Company's steamer *Princess of Wales* entered service in 1896. She at once proved herself to be a popular vessel. Here she is seen early in her career near Whitewall Creek, on the Medway.

The *Glen Rosa* appeared at Margate in 1894. By this date she was in the ownership of the Victoria Steamboat Association. This view of Margate Jetty was taken from the paddle steamer *La Marguerite*, at about 6 p.m. on a summer day as the vessel left for London. The *Glen Rosa* is about to take up the vacated berth and embark passengers for Ramsgate and Deal. The distinctive twin funnels of the paddle steamer *India* can also be seen.

VICTORIA STEAMBOAT ASSOCIATION, LTD.

THE " GLEN ROSA "
(Captain R. T. READER, late of the Steamship " India ")

LEAVES (weather and other circumstances permitting) **Margate Jetty Extension** daily at 11 a.m. and 3 p.m. for a

TWO HOURS TRIP TO SEA.
FARE 1s. 6d. CHILDREN HALF-PRICE.

The "GLEN ROSA" leaves Margate Jetty daily for

RAMSGATE AND DEAL.
at 6.15 p.m.

FARES:—DEAL ... ... Saloon, Single, 2s.
RAMSGATE ... Saloon, Single, 1s, 6d.
,, ... Fore Cabin, Single, 1s.

For further information apply at the Company's Offices, the Jetty, or Dunn's Parade Restaurant.

W. J. DUNN, Agent.

This advert from the Margate press shows the range of services provided by the *Glen Rosa* during August 1894.

Not all vessels appearing on the Thames met with success. In August 1887 the *Bonnie Doon* was chartered for Thames services to Gravesend, Sheerness and Clacton. Despite the efforts of Captain Mason and his crew, the vessel's services were not well managed, debts mounted and a writ was issued. The *Bonnie Doon* returned to her West Country owners where she was to give many years of further service. She is seen here on the South Coast much later in her career.

The General Steam Navigation Company had five paddle steamers built for Thames excursion services in the years following 1887. Known as the 'classical birds', they were all built by J. Scott, at Kinghorn, Fife. This view is of the first of them, *Halcyon*, at Great Yarmouth, *c.*1890.

The *Clacton Belle* was built for the London, Woolwich and Clacton-on-Sea Steamboat Company – usually referred to as the Belle Steamers – by Denny's at Dumbarton. She entered service in the summer of 1890 on the route from London to Clacton, sailing from Old Swan Pier. For this she required a telescopic funnel, which is clearly seen in this view taken during her builder's trials. The *Clacton Belle* was the first of the famous Belle Steamers.

The first-class dining saloon of the *Clacton Belle* photographed in 1890 by her builders. Inside views of Thames paddle steamers are very rare.

The *Woolwich Belle* was the second of the Belle Steamers to be built by Denny's at Dumbarton. Launched in 1891, she was originally intended for work on the Ipswich-Clacton service, but the demand in London was such that she began her career on the Thames in support of the *Clacton Belle*. Her original telescopic funnel is clearly visible in this early photograph.

The *Oriole* was the third of the General Steam Navigation Company's 'classical birds' and entered service in 1888. These five vessels gave the GSNC more operational scope, which is reflected in this photograph showing her at Ha'penny Pier, Harwich. On this occasion the *Oriole* may have been on a charter, as GSNC vessels of this type did not normally visit Harwich.

In the summer of 1889, the paddle steamer *Laverock* entered service. She was the fourth 'classical bird' to be built and was used on a wide variety of summer services. She is seen here at Great Yarmouth towards the end of her career, during the Edwardian period.

The *Lord of the Isles*, built in 1877, was the major rival to the *Clacton Belle* when the latter entered service. The *Lord of the Isles* was said to 'sit on the water like a duck and her whole design was a harmony without a single jarring note.' She had previously seen service on the Clyde and her new Thames owners, the Victoria Steamboat Association, adopted the colours of her previous operators, the Glasgow & Inverary Steamboat Company, for their own use.

The London Boat, Gorleston-on-Sea.

The *Mavis* was the second of the General Steam Navigation Company's 'classical birds' and entered service in 1888. She was widely used on the services to Thanet and later, to Great Yarmouth. She is seen here leaving Gorleston-on-Sea, *c*.1900. Although always popular, the five 'classical birds' were soon to be outclassed by other vessels appearing in the colours of rival companies.

The *Victoria* appeared on the Thames in 1894. Built in Scotland in 1886, she was said by some to have been the first Clyde steamer to have been fitted with electric light. Her Thames owners were the London & East Coast Express Steamship Company – in effect part of the Victoria Steamboat Association. A large vessel, *Victoria* replaced the *Glen Rosa* on the Great Yarmouth to Harwich service in 1894 but, after one season, she was found to be more profitably employed on the Thames itself.

THE FAST AND POWERFUL SALOON STEAMER

VICTORIA.

WILL Run Daily (Fridays excepted) between Yarmouth, Harwich and London,

TAKING IN PASSENGERS AT LOWESTOFT.

Daily Trips to Harwich and back. London Passengers will meet the S. Koh-i-Noor at Harwich.

David Cook's Yawl, Courage-sans-peur, will convey Passengers at 10.15 a.m. Daily (weather permitting), and land Passengers each Evening from the steamer.

Further particulars of David Cook, Boatman to the Victoria Steamboat Association, Bathing Machines, North Beach, Lowestoft.   (5093

This advert for the *Victoria* appeared in the Lowestoft Journal in July 1894. In the years before 1902, the London steamers stopped off Lowestoft and passengers could be embarked or disembarked from small boats. This was by prior arrangement and at extra cost. It is also likely that vessels stopped at Aldeburgh and Southwold, where it appears there were similar arrangements.

In 1892, the ambitious Victoria Steamboat Association had the magnificent *Koh-i-Noor* built by Fairfields on the Clyde, expressly for Thames' services. She set a new standard in 'luxury' and safety. She is seen here leaving Clacton for Harwich, probably during her first Thames season in the summer of 1892.

The *Koh-i-Noor* seen in 1893 as she approaches a crowded Ha'penny Pier, Harwich, after the journey from London. Here she would have transferred passengers to the *Glen Rosa* for the journey north to Great Yarmouth.

The power of the *Koh-i-Noor* can be seen in this early photograph, taken while she was still in the ownership of the Victoria Steamboat Association. The *Koh-i-Noor* was almost wrecked on her delivery voyage in 1892, when, in thick fog, she ran onto rocks on the Welsh coast. Only her robust construction saved her and the press made much mention of her safety features.

The *London Belle* was Belle Steamers' reply to the dominance of the *Koh-i-Noor* on the Essex services. Built by Denny's, the contract for her construction specifically stated that she was to be able to beat the *Koh-i-Noor* for speed and it is recorded that she met this requirement. The *London Belle* sailed on her maiden trip to Clacton and Harwich on 20 May 1893 and from that date she was almost continually employed on the Essex services. This rare photograph was taken during her trials on the Clyde in 1893 and shows clearly the distinctive bow-wave thrown up by the vessel, as she cut through the water at speeds up to 19 knots.

The first class lounge of the *London Belle* looking forward towards the glass doors that were etched with the company's crest. The tables and chairs were of mahogany and finished in 'plush velvet'. The ceiling skylight was of 'cathedral glass' and throughout the vessel was 'electrically lit'. This photograph originates from her builders and was taken shortly before delivery in 1893.

One of the lesser known Thames captains, was Captain Rattle of the paddle steamer *La Belgique* c.1897. *La Belgique* was intended to partner *La Marguerite* on the London, Kent and European services. Financial difficulties curtailed her Thames career after one season.

Captain Owen, one of the most renowned of the Thames paddle steamer captains, is seen aboard his vessel *La Marguerite*, c.1897, while in the employ of the Victoria Steamboat Association. This was certainly a prestigious command for a relatively young man.

The *Royal Sovereign* was built by Fairfields as a near sistership to the *Koh-i-Noor*. She was mortgaged from her builders by Palace Steamers, part of the Victoria Steamboat Association, and it is likely that she was built to counter the threat of the *London Belle*. Her construction may also reflect rivalry between the Clyde shipbuilders. The *Royal Sovereign* entered service on the run to Kent on the same day and at the same time as the *London Belle* sailed for Essex. Here she is seen from Southend Pier through the camera of Sydney Renall, *c*.1899.

In 1894, the Victoria Steamboat Association introduced *La Marguerite* to the Thames. Mortgaged from her builders, Fairfields, and named after the daughter of the VSA's manager, Arnold Williams, *La Marguerite* was an enormous vessel, over 330 feet in length. Her services were intended to compete with those of the General Steam Navigation Company to Belgium and France. She is seen here running her builder's trials in 1894. *La Marguerite* entered service to Boulogne on 23 June that same year.

It was common practice before the turn of the century for ships' captains to profit from a 'Benefit Night'. This advert appeared in the Kent press on 11 August 1894. How much Captain Owen benefited is not recorded.

After the introduction of the *London Belle* to the Thames, Belle Steamers were able to send the *Woolwich Belle* to the River Orwell. She then began a service from Ipswich to Clacton via Harwich. The *Woolwich Belle* is pictured here at Ipswich, early in her career, still carrying her telescopic funnel.

The *Woolwich Belle* is seen off the original Walton Pier soon after beginning her Ipswich to Clacton service. Walton's original pier was too short to allow berthing except at high water. The date of the photograph is unknown but must be before 1898.

Built expressly for Belle Steamers' projected Thanet services, the *Southend Belle* is seen during builder's trials on the Clyde during the late spring of 1895. While on an excursion during August 1896, the *Southend Belle* became the first Belle Steamer to enter Great Yarmouth. The postcard was published in 1905 by Valentines of Dundee.

The *Walton Belle* was built, like all the Belle Steamers, by Denny's of Dumbarton. It was with this vessel that the ambitious company intended to extend their services to Great Yarmouth in 1897 and so challenge the last monopoly of the General Steam Navigation Company. This picture shows the *Walton Belle* leaving the River Yare, c.1899.

The *Yarmouth Belle* entered service in 1898. This vessel enabled the Belle Steamers to improve their services to Great Yarmouth by removing the need for passengers to change boats at Clacton or Walton. Also, it allowed scope for more financially lucrative charters and further excursions. This early photograph probably dates from c.1898. The lack of passengers is interesting: it may be that the vessel was on trials or on her delivery voyage.

The General Steam Navigation Company responded to the Belle Steamers' threat to their Thames excursion services by ordering the *Eagle* from Gourlay Brothers of Dundee. This was the third 'Eagle' the company had owned and she entered service on the Kent run in the summer of 1898. She was the first of the famed 'Eagle Steamers' which became so well known in the following decades.

The final and perhaps the finest Belle Steamer, was the *Southwold Belle*. She was an improved version of the *Yarmouth Belle* and entered service during the summer of 1900. She was extensively employed on the long east coast service, but was also available for charters. This photograph shows her running trials on the Clyde during the late spring of 1900.

The General Steam Navigation Company's steamer *Halcyon*, c.1890. During her early years of service, the *Halcyon* provided excursions to Boulogne. She is pictured here entering the French port on an excursion, probably from Kent. *Halcyon*'s colour scheme is unusual and appears only to have been used briefly, before her owner's reverted to a traditional black hull, white superstructure and buff funnel.

Two

A Journey Through the Heyday of the Thames Paddle Steamer: 1900-1914

This photograph, taken soon after the turn of the century, shows the New Palace Steamer's *Royal Sovereign*, her funnels partially retracted, passing under Tower Bridge on her way to Kent. Astern of her, the *London Belle* can just be seen on the morning service to Clacton-on-Sea and Walton-on-the-Naze.

A crowded *Royal Sovereign* leaves Old Swan Pier for the Thanet resorts, *c*.1900. Her funnels have been retracted and her mast lowered, to enable her to pass under London Bridge. Old Swan Pier was the starting point for all Victoria Steamboat Association vessels and New Palace Steamers, with the exception of *La Marguerite*.

The *London Belle* at Fresh Wharf, as depicted on a Belle Steamer postcard. These cards were very popular and were bought on board the ship. In 1907 the set of seven Belle Steamers cost 6d (2.5 pence). Today they are commonly found, and the message on the reverse can make fascinating reading. The size of the *London Belle* often resulted in part of the vessel being under the bridge arch and, in order to help this, the *London Belle* was originally fitted with a hinged mast.

In this view of the Pool of London, the *Yarmouth Belle* is seen just after leaving Fresh Wharf, on the journey downstream, *c.*1904. This vessel was used widely on the Essex and long East Coast service. The Thames was a very crowded waterway and collisions were frequent. Damage caused by the wash of passing paddle steamers was also commonly reported in the press throughout this period.

The *London Belle* photographed at Fresh Wharf – also called London Bridge Wharf – after her return from the Essex resorts, c.1905. The gangway is in place and disembarkation will soon commence. The large number of police present may reflect the need to maintain order, as there was often a considerable level of drunkenness after a long trip. It may also be an attempt to deter pickpockets who were commonly found on board.

The *Southwold Belle* moored at Fresh Wharf after 1900. The tower of St Magnus the Martyr, one of Sir Christopher Wren's City churches, can clearly be seen. Behind that is the monument to the Great Fire of London.

The site of Fresh Wharf photographed in May 1995. The contrast with the earlier photographs is marked. Only HMS *Belfast* and the visiting *Jeremiah O'Brien*, provide passengers on the passing pleasure boat with points of nautical interest.

Another view of the site of Fresh Wharf photographed in May 1995. London Bridge, John Rennie's great masterpiece, has been replaced, as have the distinctive riverside buildings. Although dwarfed by the new buildings, the tower of St Magnus the Martyr can still be seen.

The early photographers set up their cameras on tripods and usually took a number of photographs from the one spot. At Tower Bridge the camera has caught the General Steam Navigation Company's *Eagle* on her way to Margate and Ramsgate. Out of the picture, but also photographed that day, was the *London Belle en route* to the Essex resorts, *c.*1902.

At another time, from the same place, the camera catches the *Southwold Belle*, probably on the morning service to Great Yarmouth.

TOWER BRIDGE, LONDON

The *Southend Belle* was built for the Margate service and for many years was known as the 'Husbands' Boat'. She ran an express service to Margate and Ramsgate on Saturday afternoons, leaving London at 2 p.m. In this way, men finishing work at lunchtime could join their families on the coast that same evening, at about 6.20 p.m. This photograph was taken after 1912.

HUSBANDS' BOAT.

The "SOUTHEND BELLE," Express to MARGATE & Back

Every SATURDAY AFTERNOON from the 29th JUNE until 7th SEPTEMBER inclusive.

	p.m.
Leaving **Fresh Wharf, London Bridge, at**	**2. 0**
FENCHURCH STREET, *via* Tilbury (see page 15) 2.53	
Tilbury	**3.50**
Arriving at **Margate about**	**6.20**
Leaving **Margate at**	**6.30**
Arriving at **Tilbury** { Where all passengers disembark, and are conveyed by train to Fenchurch Street, third class, free of charge, provided they exchange their Boat Returns for Rail Tickets on the Steamer ... ... } **about**	**9.30**

This advert for the 'Husbands' Boat' was found in the Belle Steamers guidebook for 1907.

37

1001. Southend Belle. P.C.

After leaving the Pool of London, the steamers arrived at Greenwich. This was always a busy pier and a favourite place for photographers. Here the *Southwold Belle* is seen leaving on her way to North Woolwich and Tilbury, *c*.1906.

"Yarmouth Belle."

The industrial background of the Thames was not thought appropriate for holiday postcards and Edwardian photographers blocked out the gasholders and chimneys, preferring instead to create a seascape. This is the same view of the *Southwold Belle* at Greenwich as depicted above. Note that in both cases the photographer has incorrectly identified the vessel – a common mistake at the time!

The *Yarmouth Belle*, also photographed as she leaves Greenwich, *c*.1906. Although the narrow congested waters of the upper Thames often required the paddle steamers to reverse upstream using their bow rudders, it is likely that, in this case, the *Yarmouth Belle* is reversing to clear the pier, and will soon move forward.

The *Southwold Belle* at Greenwich, *c*. 1906. The striking similarity between the Belle Steamers is evident when comparing this photograph of the *Southwold Belle* with that, above, of her near sister, *Yarmouth Belle*.

The river steamer *Vanbrugh* was built for the ill-fated London County Council steamboat services in 1905. Although best thought of as 'river buses', these steamers would also transport 'excursionists' from the smaller river piers to those frequented by the bigger boats. *Vanbrugh* was sold to French interests, for use on the Seine, during the summer of 1909. This type of photograph is usually associated with a vessel's entry into service and would probably date from 1905.

Another of the smaller river steamers, in the colours of the Victoria Steamboat Association, passes St Paul's Wharf in the City of London. This pier was used by some of the larger Victoria Steamboat Association vessels when they were out of service. Old Swan Pier, like Fresh Wharf, could become very crowded and space was always a consideration.

Built for the London County Council steamboat services in 1905, the *Edmund Ironside* is seen as she departs from Greenwich. As the photograph suggests, this vessel ran services from Kew to Greenwich. In 1909 the vessel was sold to interests in what is now Iraq and her subsequent history is unknown.

Greenwich Pier on 23 February 1987. The paddle steamers have long gone and small motor vessels have become commonplace on the river. The nature of excursions has also changed; here the 127-ton *Swanage Queen* awaits an evening 'Disco' cruise. By this date, *Swanage Queen*, a South Coast exile, was already thirty-nine years old.

The paddle steamer companies published a handbook each year. This is the cover of the New Palace Steamers' guide for 1901. These booklets contained a wealth of information for the 'excursionist'.

Aug 15th Dear old chap got your cigars alright will arrive next bag. I went to Southend last Sunday on this tub we were packed like herrings in a box. hoping this finds you both well yrs Scotty.

Sometimes what has been written on a postcard tells more than the picture itself. This card of the *Royal Sovereign* is typical of those that refer to the numbers found aboard steamers on the Kent services. The mention of a 'bag' may be explained by the fact that the card was sent to the British Embassy in St Petersburg. Did the diplomatic bag carry cigars?

Before the *Royal Sovereign* was towed away to Dutch ship-breakers in February 1930, this portrait of Queen Victoria was removed from her paddle box. After some time languishing in a garden, it was restored and can currently be seen with other Thames paddle steamer memorabilia, in The Felixstowe Museum at Languard Point, Suffolk.

Tilbury was an important pier for the Thames paddle steamers. Passengers could catch the train at Fenchurch Street station and join the steamers for the final part of the river trip. This cut a significant period of time off the journey and was, not surprisingly, very popular. It was from Tilbury that *La Marguerite* began her services after complaints from river users as regards her wash in the upper Thames. In this view the *London Belle* is seen on her morning service to Essex, *c*.1902.

Tilbury, photographed before 1909, with the Gravesend Ferry *Gertrude* moored alongside. *Gertrude* was a small screw steamer that transported passengers on the short journey across the river. She was later owned by the New Medway Steam Packet Company and used on services to Southend-on-Sea under the name *Rochester Queen*.

The famous paddle steamer *Golden Eagle* was built for the General Steam Navigation Company's Kent services in 1909. A magnificent vessel from Clyde shipbuilders John Brown, the *Golden Eagle* was an immediate favourite with the general public and survived on the Kent service until 1949.

PIER HEAD, SOUTHEND-ON-SEA.

Southend Pier is renowned for being the longest pleasure pier in the world. Southend-on-Sea was often the first seaside resort at which the Thames paddle steamers stopped on their journey from London, and it was frequented by many different companies over the years. The shallow water necessitated the long pier and a tramway was constructed for the benefit of visitors. Here the *Golden Eagle* is seen leaving for Kent sometime after 1909.

With steam pouring from her exhausts and capstan, the beautiful *Koh-i-Noor* is seen through the camera of Sydney Renall, as she prepares to moor at Southend in 1902. The *Koh-i-Noor*' Thames career was relatively short, ending in 1914. She was broken up immediately after the First World War.

In another photograph taken by Renall, the *London Belle* is seen returning to Southend with passengers from Clacton, c.1906. Others will now join the vessel for the trip to London. The crowded first class promenade deck contrasts with the forward 'well deck'. The low forward accommodation could be very wet, even in a moderate sea, and the company encouraged passengers to pay extra and 'go up top'.

Unlike other areas in which paddle steamers operated, photographs taken on board Thames paddle steamers are relatively rare, particularly before the First World War. This early view, again by Renall, shows a group of his friends on a cross-Channel excursion aboard *La Marguerite* in the summer of 1901.

The sheer size of *La Marguerite* can again be appreciated in this deck view, again taken in 1901. It was said at the time that everything on the ship was 'of giant proportions' and that sadly included her coal bill. She remained on the Thames until 1903 and then moved to North Wales, where she remained running excursions until September 1925. She was broken up at Briton Ferry later that same year.

In a photograph associated with the deck views seen earlier, *La Marguerite* is photographed approaching Southend Pier in the summer of 1901.

The reduction in the size of the Victoria Steamboat Association's businesses and the subsequent formation of New Palace Steamers in April 1895, resulted in the sale of the *Lord of the Isles*. She remained on the Thames for a few seasons under the name *Jupiter*, before returning to Scotland. *Jupiter* is seen here in the Thames estuary during September 1900.

The paddle steamer *Lady Margaret* was owned by the Medway Steam Packet Company and had been purchased in 1888 to improve the quality of their services to the Medway towns. She was a popular vessel but was sadly destroyed by fire in 1903. She is seen here approaching Southend Pier, c.1899.

The Medway Steam Packet vessel *Princess of Wales* is seen here during the summer of 1900. Built at Middlesbrough in 1896, this vessel was frequently used on the Southend to Rochester service. She was broken up in 1928.

One of the attractions of a paddle steamer trip to Rochester was the opportunity to view the fleet at Sheerness. Here, in a remarkable Renall's photograph, HMS *Nile* and other battleships of the Victorian Navy, are seen from the deck of a paddle steamer of the Medway Steam Packet Company, *c*.1899.

Another view by Renall entitled 'A trip to Sheerness'. A Royal Sovereign class battleship partially obscures an earlier 'turret ship' and a cruiser, *c*.1899.

The *London Belle*, the largest vessel in the Belle Steamer's fleet, is seen here off Southend Pier, *c.*1900. From here, passengers could transfer to smaller steamers for trips to the Medway towns.

Herne Bay Pier as seen from the paddle steamer *Cynthia*, *c.*1902. In 1899, after considerable improvements had been made to the existing pier structure, Herne Bay increased in popularity as a destination for excursions from London and Southend. Note the pier tram just visible in this photograph by Renall.

The well-known Passenger Steamer,
"CYNTHIA,"
Connected throughout with Electric Light
(CAPT. J. JONES)

WILL make the following EXCURSIONS from RAMSGATE HARBOUR (wind, weather, and other circumstances permitting):—

SUNDAY, Aug. 12.—**Trip to Sea.** Leaving Ramsgate Harbour at 11 a.m. Returning about One o'clock. FARE 1s. 6d.

MONDAY, Aug. 13.—**Boulogne.** Leaving Ramsgate, 10: Deal, 10.30. Returning same day. Passengers are allowed about 2½ hours ashore.

TUESDAY, Aug. 14.—**Boulogne.** Leaving Ramsgate, 10; Deal, 10.30. Returning same day. Passengers are allowed about 2½ hours ashore.

WEDNESDAY, Aug. 15.—**Deal, Dover,** and **Folkestone.** Leaving Ramsgate, 11.30; Deal, 12; Dover, 1.15. Returning from Dover at 4 p.m.

THURSDAY, Aug. 16—**Boulogne.** Leaving Ramsgate, 10; Deal, 10.30. Returning same day. Passengers are allowed about 2½ hours ashore.

FRIDAY, Aug. 17.—**Trip to the Downs.** Leaving Ramsgate Harbour at 11.30 a.m Fare 1s.

A Special Excursion **Around the Goodwins** with Members of the Sanitary Inspectors' Association. leaving Ramsgate Harbour at 3 p.m Any person can join this Excursion. Fare 2s. 6d. Tickets to be obtained at the Office, East Pier, Ramsgate.

SATURDAY, Aug. 18.—**Deal** and **Dover.** Leaving Ramsgate, 11 30; Deal, 12. Returning from Dover at 4 p.m.

LUNCHEONS, TEAS, &c., on Board, at popular prices.

AGENTS:—Mr. P. PEPPERELL, 6, Ethelbert-road, Margate, and at Ramsgate; Mr. ROGERS, care of Messrs. Hammond, opposite the Pier, Deal; Mr. CONSTANT, 4, Beach-street, Dover.

NOTICE.—Intending passengers from Margate for Boulogne by this well-known Steamer will be in time to join her at Ramsgate by leaving Margate at 8.55 a.m. (L.C.D.R.) or 9.35 a.m. (S.E.R.)

Intending passengers from Margate for Deal, Dover, and Folkestone, by this well-known Steamer, will be in time to join her by leaving Margate at 10.35 a.m. (L.C.D.R.) or 10.30 (S.E.R.)

FARES:	Single.	Return.
Ramsgate to Deal	1s. 0d.	1s. 6d.
Ramsgate to Dover	2s. 0d.	2s. 6d.
Ramsgate to Folkestone	2s. 6d.	3s. 6d.
Deal to Dover	—	1s. 6d.
Deal to Folkestone	—	2s. 6d.
Dover to Folkestone	1s. 0d.	1s. 6d.
Ramsgate and Deal to Boulogne	—	6s. 0d.
Children	—	4s. 0d.

The paddle steamer *Cynthia* is one of the lesser known Thames paddle steamers. Built in 1892, she was a small excursion steamer that ran sea trips from the Kent resorts and Southend. This advert from the Kent press gives the range of excursions available in 1894. Soon after this *Cynthia* left the Thames and went north, but returned again in about 1900. She later spent some time at Hastings before embarking on a nomadic career that ended when she was wrecked at Kingstown, Ireland, during 1934.

The smartly painted paddle steamer *Cynthia* is seen leaving Southend Pier. Little is written about the *Cynthia*, but this photograph was taken during her second period on the Thames during the summer of 1902.

This superb photograph by Sydney Renall gives us a unique insight into a Thames excursion to Herne Bay, on board the paddle steamer *Cynthia*, during what is believed to be the summer of 1902. A fiddle-player provides entertainment but at least one passenger prefers to sleep. The gentleman with the pipe is recorded as being William Baker of Southend.

The 'double-ended' paddle steamer *Essex* is more usually associated with the River Orwell than the Thames. Built in 1896 for Great Eastern Railway services between Harwich and Ipswich, *Essex* was sold in 1913 for use as a ferry between Southend and Sheerness. She moved to the Humber in 1916 and then to the Mediterranean in 1918. Her ultimate fate is unknown. *Essex* is seen here on the Orwell at the turn of the century.

With the naval fleet across the water at Chatham and Sheerness, there were always plenty of sailors attracted to the entertainments offered by Southend. The vessels of the Medway Steam Packet fleet transported them across the estuary and back. This view shows 'matelots' heading back to the pier head, *c*.1900.

The *City of Rochester* was built in 1904 for the Thames services of the Medway Steam Packet Company. She was a great favourite with passengers on the Southend to Sheerness service until her loss during the Second World War. This photograph was taken before 1911.

The *Mermaid* was another of the smaller Thames paddle steamers that operated as far downstream as Southend. Built at Poplar in 1891, she is seen here during the Edwardian period while in the ownership of the London Steamboat Company. After a varied career in both England and Ireland, during which she was commandeered by the Irish Free State Army, she was scrapped at Preston in late 1927.

Margate Jetty was an impressive structure and was used by steamers from many different companies over the years. Here, in this Edwardian view, the General Steam Navigation Company's paddle steamer *Oriole* approaches with passengers from London. After the *Eagle* entered service in 1898, the *Oriole* was used as a supplementary vessel on this route, sometimes beginning her journey at Tilbury.

Margate photographed after 1909 with the 'Jetty' in the distance. The General Steam Navigation Company's vessel *Golden Eagle* has just departed and her place is about to be taken by Belle Steamers' *Southend Belle*, which has probably come from Ramsgate.

Margate Sands as seen in the New Palace Steamers' guide for 1903.

Koh-i-Noor enters Ramsgate before 1910. The most obvious difference between *Koh-i-Noor* and *Royal Sovereign* was the positioning of the latter's funnels some twelve feet further forward than her sister. As a result of this, *Royal Sovereign* presented a more balanced profile.

The General Steam Navigation Company 'experimented' with turbine propulsion in 1906. Built by Denny's at Dumbarton, the propeller-driven *Kingfisher* was fast and luxurious but, according to contemporary accounts, she was also a 'poor seaboat' and was sold in 1912. Used exclusively on the continental services from London, she is seen here at Dover. The date of the picture is unknown.

Excursions could take the paddle steamers away from the Thames completely. The Victorian and Edwardian naval reviews at Portsmouth were just such occasions. This very unusual photograph shows a crowded *Southwold Belle* at Southsea. Research would suggest that this visit was probably for the Coronation Review of 1902. Although the coronation was cancelled due to the King's illness, the charters were taken up and at least two Belle Steamers went to Southampton.

The attractions of continental beaches were clearly depicted in the New Palace Steamers' guide for 1903. *La Marguerite* would take you there for 11s 6d (57.5p) return!

SAILINGS BETWEEN
London, Walton, Felixstowe, Southwold, Lowestoft, Gorleston and Yarmouth.

Up and Down THROUGH STEAMERS,
"SOUTHWOLD BELLE" or "YARMOUTH BELLE,"

On the 6th and 7th JULY, and DAILY (except FRIDAYS),
from the 13th JULY to 7th SEPTEMBER inclusive.

The Yarmouth Local Steamer will run on Fridays between 19th July and 30th August, both inclusive, connecting with the 9.0 a.m. Steamer to Walton, as shown on page 8.

NOTE—A Special Express Relief Steamer will run to Gorleston and Yarmouth on Saturday, 3rd August, leaving Fresh Wharf at 8.45 a.m., but there will be no Up Steamer from Yarmouth, Gorleston, Lowestoft, or Southwold on this date.

DOWN JOURNEY.

	a.m.
Leaving	
London Bridge (Fresh Wharf)	**9.45**
FENCHURCH STREET, *via* Tilbury (see page 15)... { Weekdays 10.14 / Sundays 10.15 }	
ST. PANCRAS, *via* Tilbury (see page 16) ... { Weekdays 9.35 / Sundays 9 55 }	
LIVERPOOL STREET, *via* Woolwich (see page 17)... { Weekdays 8.21 / Sundays 9.26 }	
FENCHURCH STREET, *via* Woolwich (see page 17)... { Weekdays 9.40 / Sundays 8.52 }	
Greenwich	**10. 5**
Woolwich (North Side, G.E.Ry. Pier)	**10.30**
Tilbury { Passengers from S.E. & C. Ry., *via* Gravesend, book at the Town Pier, or at the Office of the Company's Agent, and cross by the Ferry free of charge ... ... } ...	**11.45**
	p.m.
Walton	**3.30**
Felixstowe (New Pier)	**4. 0**
Southwold	**5.45**
Lowestoft (Claremont Pier)	**6.30**
Arriving	
Gorleston	**7.30**
Yarmouth (Town Hall Quay) ... ... **about**	**8. 0**

UP JOURNEY.

	a.m.
Leaving	
Yarmouth (Town Hall Quay) (Saturday, 3rd August, excepted)	**9.15**
Gorleston	**9.30**
Lowestoft (Claremont Pier)	**10.20**
Southwold	**11. 0**
	p.m.
Felixstowe (New Pier)	**12.30**
Walton (where Passengers for Clacton, Harwich, & Ipswich change)	**1.30**
Southend	**4. 0**
Tilbury (where Passengers for L.T. & S.Ry. & M.Ry. disembark)	**5. 0**
Woolwich (North) (where Passengers for G.E.Ry. disembark)	**6. 0**
Greenwich	**6.30**
Arriving	
London Bridge ... ... **about**	**7. 0**

This timetable from the Belle Steamers' guide of 1907, shows the range of services given by the company at the height of their prosperity.

The *Yarmouth Belle* is depicted on a popular postcard of the time. The vessel was again photographed at Greenwich and the background obliterated c.1906.

This view from the stern of the *Yarmouth Belle* is unique. It was taken on Saturday, 29 July 1905, by an unknown photographer, as the vessel steamed north along the Essex coast towards Clacton. Other photographs in this series suggest that the ultimate destination was Great Yarmouth. Thames sailing barges can be seen in the distance.

The *Walton Belle* depicted on a Belle Steamers' postcard. The message reads: 'Upper Deck 1.15 p.m. – Am having a grand voyage. Brilliant sunshine with rather a cool wind. Steaming along steady as a rock. Am just passing the Nore. Excuse writing as they don't provide tables up on deck. – Allan. P.S. Arrived safely 9 p.m. Second half pretty rough. A.D.S.' The postmark is 23 June 1911.

This view of *Woolwich Belle* was taken some time before 1905. She has a one piece funnel but no enclosed fore-saloon. The small funnel to the right of the paddle box was the flue to the galley ranges, that were, like the ship herself, coal-fired.

This advert from 1907 gives the range of services offered by the *Woolwich Belle*. By this date the *Woolwich Belle* was regarded as Ipswich's very own vessel and her withdrawal from that station, for any reason, usually resulted in letters to the press.

THE PIER & S.S. "LONDON BELLE", CLACTON-ON-SEA.

Clacton-on-Sea developed with the growth in the popularity of seaside holidays. The paddle steamers were an essential part of this, and threats to their services were viewed very seriously by the local entrepreneurs. The original Belle Steamers' company was established in 1888, to secure steamer services to the town, using the first of their vessels, the small paddle steamer *Clacton*. This view shows the *London Belle* leaving for Walton-on-the-Naze after the turn of the century.

Landing at Clacton Pier

The crowd that awaited the arrival of the steamers can be gauged by this view of the pier head at Clacton. It was not unknown for the press of people to cause accidents and there are reports of people falling from the pier-head into the sea. The vessel shown here is the *Southend Belle*, c.1903.

Walton Pier developed after that built at Clacton. The improvements made in 1898 allowed for the mooring of two or three steamers simultaneously. It was, therefore, seen by Belle Steamers as being ideal as a meeting place for their vessels from Ipswich, Margate, Great Yarmouth and London. This caused some friction with Clacton and threats from local Clacton businesses to build a new pier. The threats came to nothing and both towns thrived. This view was probably taken around 1898 and shows four Belle Steamers.

This photograph was taken a few minutes later than the one above, at about 3.30 p.m. The advertisements at the pier entrance would suggest that this is an early view and help to identify the vessels. The *Woolwich Belle* has now moored, with what seem to be the *Yarmouth Belle*, on the left, and the *Walton Belle*, on the right, exchanging Great Yarmouth passengers. The *London Belle* has left for Southend. The new pier tramway is seen running along the left side of the structure while, in the foreground, a tram is being used as a temporary waiting room.

EMBARKING AT WALTON PIER.

On a hot summer day at Walton-on-the-Naze during the middle Edwardian period, passengers await the late afternoon departure of a Belle Steamer. It is possible that this vessel was on a special excursion, as the regular services tended to leave earlier in the afternoon. By this date, trips from Tilbury to Lowestoft were common and vessels would have left Walton at about 5.30 p.m., for the return to Southend (8 p.m.) and Gravesend (9 p.m.). It is rather unusual in views of Thames paddle steamers to see that the passengers are aware of the photographer.

In another superb view, the *Walton Belle* is seen at Walton Pier. Passengers have just landed and carry their bags with them. The ship's wheel, at the forward end of the promenade deck, was used to operate the bow rudder when the vessel was navigating in the confined waters of the upper Thames, or on the River Yare at Great Yarmouth. The photograph is undated but must originate from about 1900.

In this interesting view of the pier head at Walton, a tram appears to be undergoing some form of maintenance. Again the picture is undated but was probably taken around the year 1900.

REFRESHMENT TARIFF.

The following is the Tariff of Charges for supply of Meals and Refreshments on board the Belle Steamers:—

COLD LUNCHEONS are served in the Saloons until 12 noon.
HOT DINNERS will be served as soon after 12.30 as possible.
TEAS from 4.30 until 6.30 p.m.

On Bank Holidays and special occasions other arrangements are made.

SALOON.

	s.	d.
HOT DINNER (*ad lib.*), consisting of Soup (or Fish), Joints (boiled and roast), Two Vegetables, Sweets, Bread and Cheese, Butter and Salad	2	6
Do. do. as above, with Poultry	3	0
COLD LUNCHEON (*ad lib.*), consisting of Joints, Ham and Tongue, Potatoes, Bread and Cheese, Butter and Salad ...	2	0
Do. do. with portion of Poultry or Fish	2	6
TEA (*ad lib.*) with Watercress and Preserves	1	0
Do. do. do. do. with Shrimps	1	3
Do. do. do. do. with a portion of Meat or Fish	2	0
Do. do. do. do. with a portion of Meat and Fish	2	6

(When Poultry or Lobster is served the minimum charge will be 2s. 6d.)

FORE CABIN.

	s.	d.
HOT DINNER, consisting of a cut from the Joint (boiled or roast), Two Vegetables, Bread, Cheese, and Butter	1	6
COLD LUNCHEON, consisting of Plate of Cold Meat, Potatoes, Bread and Cheese, and Butter	1	3
TEA, plain, with Bread and Butter and Marmalade	0	9
Do. do. do. do. and Shrimps	1	0
Do. do. do. do. with a portion of Meat or Fish	1	6

TEA BARS.

FRUIT, CONFECTIONERY, and LIGHT REFRESHMENTS may be obtained at the TEA BARS, adjoining the Saloon, and in the Fore Cabin.
Tea, 3d. per cup.

WINE LIST.

	Bot. s. d.	½ Bot. s. d.		Bot. s. d.	½ Bot. s. d.
1. SHERRY—Dry Dinner ...	4 0	2 6	9. HOCK—Niersteiner	4 0	2 0
2. Amontillado	6 6	3 6	10. Rudesheimer	6 0	—
3. PORT—Fine Old ..	5 0	3 0	CHAMPAGNE—		
4. Very Old and Tawny ...	8 0	4 0	11. Coast	6 0	3 6
5. CLARET, &c.—Medoc ...	3 0	1 6	12. Moet & Chandon, W.D.S....	10 6	5 6
6. Cos d'Estournal	4 0	—	13. Giegler	12 6	6 6
7. Pontet Canet	5 0	2 6	14. Pol Roger, 1884, Cuvee N.	12 6	—
8. Beaune	4 0	2 3	15. G. H. Mumm, extra dry ...	12 6	6 6
			16. Sparkling Moselle	6 0	—

LIQUEURS—Choice Old Cognac ...	6d.	Curacoa	6d.
Chartreuse Yellow	6d.	Kummell	6d.
Benedictine ... ... 6d.			

ALES, MINERALS, & SPIRITS.

Old Scotch Whisky	4d.	Bass & Co.'s and Whitbread's Stout—	
Irish	4d.	Imp. pint 6d. ½ pint	4d.
Brandy	6d.	Soda, large bottle	4d.
Gin	4d.	Seltzer	4d.
Dry Sherry ... ... per glass	6d.	Lemonade	4d.
Amontillado	6d.	Soda and Milk ... ... 2d. &	4d.
Port	6d.	Ginger Beer ... ... 3d. &	6d.
Bass & Co.'s and Whitbread's Ale—		Cigars	3d.
Imp. pint 6d ½ pint 4d.		... ... 4d. &	6d.

The 'Refreshment Tariff' from the Belle Steamers' guide of 1907, reveals the range of food available on the paddle steamers. Such menus are typical of the time. One of the factors that exacerbated Belle Steamers' financial difficulties towards the end of the Edwardian decade, was that the catering on the vessels was tendered out to other small businesses and the large profits made from catering were therefore lost to the company.

Originally the steamers visiting Felixstowe used the small pier just inside the harbour, opposite Harwich. This was some distance from the town centre and was not felt to be best sited. In 1905 Belle Steamers opened a new pier on the seafront. Like Walton-on-the-Naze, this pier also had a tramway along one side. In this photograph the *Woolwich Belle*, under the command of Captain Holland, approaches the pier for the first time on 1 July 1905.

Felixstowe Pier was typical of the piers built by Belle Steamers in the towns north of Walton-on-the-Naze. These simple structures were primarily landing places and, as such, the mooring rights were jealously guarded. Before the First World War ships of other companies were not allowed to moor, with the result that the General Steam Navigation Company advertised 'direct' services to Great Yarmouth.

In this photograph, taken at Felixstowe soon after 1905, the *Walton Belle* arrives on her journey north to Southwold, Lowestoft and Great Yarmouth. Mooring at these very exposed pier heads was difficult, in even a moderate swell. On some days, landing was impossible and passengers were then taken on to the next pier. There, if possible, they were given the train fare to take them back to their original destination.

This rare photograph shows Southwold Pier under construction in 1899. The Belle Steamers' owners – then known as the Coast Development Company – had purchased land at Southwold. They built the Grand Hotel on the seafront and then constructed the pier a little distance away. From the pier entrance, a new road, Pier Avenue, led directly to the railway station. The remaining land was sold for the building of 'select residences'.

Southwold Pier is seen at the height of its Edwardian popularity with a Belle Steamer about to moor. This photograph would have been taken from the grounds of the Grand Hotel. Southwold was popular with 'excursionists' from Great Yarmouth and Lowestoft, as well as those from London.

The remains of Southwold Pier photographed some ninety years after the picture above. Architects, war and the ravages of the sea have all taken their toll on the Victorian structure. In 1999 work started on the restoration of the pier and there are ambitious plans for its future development.

Lowestoft's Claremont Pier was opened in May 1902. Like that at Southwold, it was a very simple pier, with a 'T' end against which a steamer could moor.

Lowestoft's Claremont Pier, seen here in July 1999, has deteriorated greatly over the years. It was last used by steamers in 1939, and today it is hard to imagine the vast numbers of people that would have used the structure on summer days before the Great War. In December 1999, the press announced plans for the refurbishment of the pier. However, for the present, with the seaward end closed to the public, the future of England's most easterly pier remains in the balance.

Journeys end... or beginning, was the entrance to the River Yare at Gorleston. Here the *Walton Belle* is seen leaving on a journey that many passengers may have come to regret making (*c*.1900). The *Walton Belle* has been using her bow rudder to come downstream from Yarmouth and is leaving backwards. Once outside, she will turn and head south, passing the coastal villages of Hopton and Corton, before reaching Lowestoft.

Passengers often wrote their postcards soon after arrival. They make interesting reading as they often refer in detail to the journeys made. This one, from August 1905, suggests the author had quite a rough passage. Others talk of crowds, 'feeding the fishes' (seasickness) and occasionally mechanical breakdowns.

The *Walton Belle* manoeuvring at 'the knuckle', Gorleston, *c.*1906. On occasions vessels turned at this point and went backwards up to Yarmouth. At other times they came downstream, misjudged the current and hit the quayside! Throughout the whole period of paddle steamer excursions, the entrance to the Yare presented problems to generations of sea-captains.

Belle Steamers began stopping at Brush Quay, Gorleston, in 1905. This was in response to local pressure from hoteliers and boarding house-keepers. Gorleston was a popular destination, but previously visitors had to disembark at Hall Quay, Great Yarmouth, and find their own way back down the river, often by small boats. This card dates from that period and shows *Southwold Belle* near the King William IV public house.

The *Southend Belle* moored at Great Yarmouth, some time after 1905. She was not commonly seen in Yarmouth, except on excursions. She was often sent on 'Race Days', when she was known as the 'Bookmakers' Boat'. Bank holidays also saw some of the larger Belle boats in the port, as the demand warranted, and the stern of another Belle Steamer can be seen in this photograph. The General Steam Navigation Company vessels usually moored a few yards further upstream, at Haven Bridge.

The General Steam Navigation Company's steamer *Halcyon*, at Haven Bridge, probably before 1904. After the completion of the East Coast piers in 1905, the GSNC found it increasingly difficult to compete with the Belle Steamers and, as the five 'Classic Birds' were gradually withdrawn, the service to Great Yarmouth became less frequent. The appearance of the *Oriole* in August 1910 marked the end of an era. In 1911, Belle Steamers had a monopoly on the Great Yarmouth service.

The front cover of the Belle Steamers' guide for 1911 shows the *Southwold Belle* near Sheerness. The company's coat of arms depicts the four areas serviced by the fleet and also where the initial company capital was raised. By this date the Belle Steamers were experiencing financial difficulties and *Southwold Belle* was withdrawn and sold after the end of the summer season.

Three
The Years of Change: 1914-1939

The outbreak of the Great War in August 1914, saw little change to the Thames paddle steamer services until the beginning of September. Then, with an uncertain future ahead, they returned to their winter moorings. The Belle Steamers went to London, from where they were later requisitioned by the Admiralty as minesweepers. *Walton Belle* became HMPMS 579 (His Majesty's Paddle Minesweeper), and is seen here in 1917 while based in Harwich. This photograph originates from a post-war booklet published by her owners.

The *Yarmouth Belle* was commissioned as HMPMS 929 in August 1915. She narrowly escaped destruction in November 1915, when the vessel working with her blew up near the Galloper. Although damaged, the *Yarmouth Belle* rescued a few lucky survivors from the cold North Sea. Commander Wegram, her commanding officer, was later awarded the DSO.

The crew of the *Yarmouth Belle*, c.1917. It was probably good fortune, as much as good seamanship, that saw all the Belle Steamers return from active service in 1919.

In 1917 the gun crew of the *Walton Belle* won an 'anti-aircraft shooting prize' while at Harwich. Research has revealed this photograph with the crew at their action stations. It was almost certainly posed for the occasion.

The crew of the *Southend Belle*, c.1917. The crews of these paddle steamers were mainly reservists. Life on these lightly-built ships was hard and in some instances, terrifyingly short. The *Southend Belle* was commissioned in April 1916 as HMPMS 532.

The *Clacton Belle*, HMPMS 930, was commissioned in August 1915. Her crew had direct contact with the enemy when she rescued sailors from a Zeppelin that had crashed in the Thames estuary in 1917. Her commanding officer, Commander Sutton-Smith, later received the DSO.

The crew of the *Clacton Belle*, c.1917.

The *Clacton Belle*, c.1917, as seen in another photograph published by the Belle Steamers after the war. A crew member poses in his kapok life jacket while, behind, the minesweeping apparatus can be seen on the quarter deck. The *Clacton Belle* was said to have destroyed some 342 mines during her wartime service.

The crew of the *London Belle*, c.1917. The *London Belle* was based at Harwich until late 1917 when she was moved to Liverpool. There she continued minesweeping until 1919. On her return to the Thames, both she and *Walton Belle* were fitted out as 'Hospital Carriers' and sent to northern Russia, via the North Cape. This journey was a remarkable achievement for a Thames paddle steamer.

Once the pride of the Victoria Steamboat Association, *La Marguerite*'s running costs were partly responsible for her owner's financial downfall. The First World War removed financial consideration and *La Marguerite*'s size and speed proved invaluable when transporting troops across the English Channel (*c.*1918). Here she is in 'dazzle-ship' camouflage. Designed by Norman Wilkinson, it was used to confuse enemy submarines.

The *Southwold Belle* had been sold and had left the Thames after the 1911 season. By the outbreak of war in 1914, she was operating in French waters under the name *Bon Voyage*. She was used to transport troops in the Mediterranean, where this photograph, thought to show her at Salonika, was taken. The date is unrecorded.

The original owners of the Belle Steamers had been placed in receivership during 1915. In 1920, some of the freshly refitted vessels were once again 'chartered' for use on the Thames. This advert relates to the summer of 1920 and refers to the booklet from which the wartime photographs were mostly extracted.

In 1919 the General Steam Navigation Company's *Golden Eagle* was again seen on the Thames. This postcard recording her wartime exploits could be bought aboard.

The Belle Steamers and the *Royal Sovereign* eventually came under the ownership of the Shankland brothers, and were once again found on their pre-war routes. This photograph of the *Royal Sovereign* dates from this period and is one of a series published by the company.

During the immediate post-war period, the distinctive tall funnel of the *Clacton Belle* was regularly seen on the long East Coast service to Great Yarmouth.

In the same series of pictures, the *Southend Belle* is viewed from a different angle.

The *London Belle*, photographed leaving Southend- on-Sea, soon after her return from war service in Russia.

S.S. Audrey. N.M.S.P.Cº
Southend to Herne Bay daily

The Medway Steam Packet Company did not survive the First World War. In 1919 a new company was formed that took over the ships and was appropriately named The New Medway Steam Packet Company. One of their 'new' vessels was the small paddle steamer *Audrey*. She is seen here in the Thames estuary, *c.*1923.

Mishaps affecting Belle Steamers were comparatively rare. However, in 1922 *Clacton Belle* suffered mechanical problems with her steering mechanism, shortly after leaving Great Yarmouth. She is seen here being towed backwards into the Yare. The two lifeboats at the stern were Board of Trade requirements, following the *Titanic* disaster in 1912.

Following her breakdown in 1922, the *Clacton Belle* negotiates the river bend at Gorleston and passes Brush Quay, under the tow of a Yarmouth paddle tug.

The *Woolwich Belle* had been laid up during the hostilities. Subsequently, she returned to her builders at Dumbarton and was refitted. She reappeared in 1922 under the name *Queen of the South*. This photograph shows her on the Clyde with a new short funnel. This was unsatisfactory and was lengthened before she returned south – not to the Thames, but initially to the South Coast.

The *Walton Belle* was again regularly seen at Great Yarmouth in the early 1920s.

The *Queen of the South* was purchased by the New Medway Steam Packet Company in 1924 and was widely used on services to Essex and Kent.

The New Medway Steam Packet Company ordered the *Medway Queen* from Ailsa Shipbuilding & Engineering Company at Troon. She was the first purpose-built Thames paddle steamer since the *Golden Eagle* in 1909 and arrived on the River Medway in time for the 1924 season.

Holiday memories of a 'sea trip' taken long ago.
A family photograph taken on board *Medway Queen*, c.1925.

New technology and an increasingly discerning public saw the General Steam Navigation Company order the *Crested Eagle* from Samuel White's yard at Cowes. Oil-fired boilers and a 'luxurious' interior in a 'modern style', made her a great favourite with passengers and her owners. Soon after entering service in 1925, she became known as the 'Greyhound of the Thames'. She is seen here on trials in the Solent in 1925.

In December 1925 the New Medway Steam Packet Company purchased *Walton Belle*. She was renamed *Essex Queen* and put on the Margate service. She is seen here, soon after her change of name, on what is probably a firm's charter.

Belle Steamers employed the much respected Captain Owen, as one of their senior captains. He is seen here on the bridge of the *Southend Belle* in 1928. Is this the same Captain Owen who commanded *La Marguerite* in 1894? This photograph originates from the personal collection belonging to ship owner Robert Shankland's family.

In 1928 the New Medway Steam Packet Company purchased two ex-naval Ascot Class minesweepers from their respective ship-breakers. Both were refitted and put onto Thames services. In this photograph a smart *Queen of Kent* is seen in a composite photograph, with herself as the more drab HMS *Atherstone*, c.1929.

The *Queen of Thanet* had been built as the minesweeper HMS *Melton* in 1916. Once refitted, she and her sister gave their new owners the opportunity to offer continental excursions. She is seen here leaving Southend-on-Sea.

As a company, Belle Steamers ceased to operate after the close of the 1928 season and the four remaining vessels were sold. So ended an era that had begun in 1890. Even at that late date, photographers were still confusing the vessels. This is not the *Clacton Belle*, but the *Walton Belle* photographed off Southend Pier, c.1928.

The *Clacton Belle* was considered too old for modernization, and was sold to ship-breakers Thomas Ward at Grays, Essex, where she was photographed in 1929.

The wharf of ship-breakers Thomas Ward at Grays, Essex, in 1929. Perhaps this is the last photograph of the saloon deck that had been a feature of the *Clacton Belle*'s construction. Ward's were to make short work of her and the larger *London Belle*, which also ended her days at the same ship-breakers.

The *Royal Sovereign* was also sold after the 1928 season ended. Rather surprisingly, she was purchased by the General Steam Navigation Company and sailed for them in 1929 on the Margate service. After that she was sold for scrap. She is seen here passing under Tower Bridge during 1929, her final year of service.

The *Queen of the South* was stationed at Great Yarmouth during 1929. One of her engineers was Billy King, who is pictured here by her paddle-box, posing for a family photograph during that summer. When the *Queen of the South* was withdrawn, Billy remained in Great Yarmouth and found other work.

Clacton Pier with the *Queen of the South* off the pier head, *c.*1929. The *Queen of the South* remained in service until 1931, when she was laid up on the Medway. She was towed to ship-breakers Thomas Ward at Grays in July 1932.

New tastes in music and the fashion for night-clubs resulted in the *Showboat* appearing on the Thames in 1932. With decks modified to allow dancing, a theatre and a restaurant, *Showboat* cruised the upper Thames. In 1933 she was anchored off Margate, but conditions were not suitable and she soon moved to the shelter of Shoreham, where this photograph was taken in 1933. Originally built as the *Alexandra* in 1879, the *Showboat* went to the breakers in 1934.

The General Steam Navigation Company introduced the large *Royal Eagle* to the Thames in May 1932. She was a replacement for both the *Eagle*, broken up after the 1928 season, and the *Royal Sovereign*. Built specifically for Thames services, the *Royal Eagle* was an immediate success on the London-to-Southend and Margate service.

The main dining saloon of the *Royal Eagle*, c.1932.

In 1929 *Southend Belle* had been purchased by the owners of Clacton Pier, to run services to the town from London. She was renamed *Laguna Belle* and is pictured here against Clacton Pier, *c.*1933.

The expansion of the New Medway Steam Packet Company continued in late 1933, with the purchase of the *Clacton Queen*. Originally built in 1897, for services to the Isle of Wight, as the *Duchess of Kent*, she is pictured here at Ipswich, *c.*1934.

"GOLDEN EAGLE"
CAPTAIN W. SERGENT

The famous early excursion
steamer at very reduced fares.
Known, at Margate, as the
"Happy Ship".

"ISLE OF ARRAN"
Afternoon Cruises through
the Great London Docks
on Wednesdays & Saturdays
see opposite page.

This page from the General Steam Navigation Company's guide for 1933, reflects the continued popularity of the *Golden Eagle*. The older *Isle of Arran* had been purchased that year for cruises through the London Docks.

After the demise of Belle Steamers, the *Yarmouth Belle* had been purchased by the New Medway Steam Packet Company and renamed *Queen of Southend*. By this date they were advertised as the 'Queen Line'. In 1935 she was modernized and her appearance changed to that seen in this photograph which was taken near Southend-on-Sea probably in 1936.

M.V.. QUEEN OF THE CHANNEL.
Queen Line Rochester.

The motor vessel *Queen of the Channel* appeared in 1935. She was owned by the New Medway Steam Packet Company, and was constructed to the highest specifications by Denny's of Dumbarton. Large motor vessels such as this, were to threaten the very survival of the traditional Thames paddle steamer. The *Queen of the Channel* was the first of three large motor vessels built for Thames services during the 1930s.

The graceful lines of the *Lady Orme* were seen briefly at Ramsgate during 1936. Built in 1888 as the *Fusilier*, she spent forty-six years in Scotland, before embarking on a career that involved one season on the Thames. She was finally scrapped in 1939.

Tower Bridge opens for the *Laguna Belle* on a trip to Southend and Clacton in September 1934.

The *Golden Eagle* passes the *Laguna Belle* in the lower Thames, in September 1934.

Photographed near Tilbury, *c.*1934, the *Laguna Belle* passes what is believed to be the motor vessel *Pacific Pioneer*, moving slowly upstream to discharge her cargo. The *Pacific Pioneer* was torpedoed in the Atlantic during July 1942.

Deck view on board the *Royal Eagle* in the Thames, *c*.1936. The portly figure of Captain Branthwaite can be seen on the bridge.

The leisurely pace of the paddle steamer gave the 'excursionist' time to talk, relax and enjoy a few hours away from the rush of everyday-life. Personal photographs such as this are a reminder of such times. Mr William Hunter, on the left, and Mr Gordon Prynne, on the right, are seen on board the *Essex Queen* in the Thames estuary, *c*.1928.

Breakdowns were rare but did occur. In this photograph passengers await the arrival of the *Isle of Arran*, after their vessel, the *Royal Eagle*, had developed mechanical problems in the lower Thames, while on passage to Southend-on-Sea. The exact date is unknown, but is thought to be 1935.

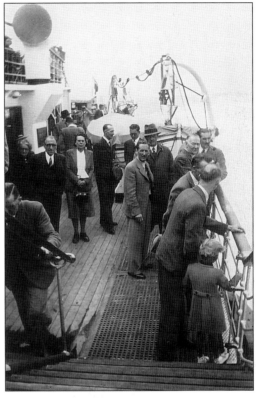

Passengers with return tickets to Tower Pier are closely supervised as they pass from the *Royal Eagle* to the smaller *Isle of Arran*, for the return to London. Those remaining on the *Royal Eagle* had to wait a few more hours before setting foot ashore in Southend-on-Sea.

Why Go to America ? ? ?

GO TO MARGATE

AND

DRINK
JENNER'S
GOLDEN ALE

ON BOARD THE

" GOLDEN EAGLE "

JENNER'S BREWERY
SOUTHWARK

ESTᴰ· NEARLY 150 YEARS

This advert from the General Steam Navigation Company's guide for 1931 serves to remind us that, as in earlier decades, the consumption of alcohol remained an important source of income for the Thames paddle steamer operators.

In 1938 continental excursions were offered from Great Yarmouth and Lowestoft to Ostend. This was in addition to those from London. These 'day trips' were not run by the traditional paddle steamer but the new motor vessel the *Royal Sovereign*. She is pictured to the right of the *Queen of the Channel* in Ostend during 1938.

In June 1936 the *Queen of Kent* reopened the Great Yarmouth service, which had hitherto lapsed. She ran daily (Fridays excepted) to Clacton-on-Sea. She is seen here leaving Gorleston, c.1936; by this date her owners were under the control of the General Steam Navigation Company.

Subject to alteration.

EAGLE STEAMERS — 1939 PROGRAMME

Services from LONDON to—
Southend, Margate, Ramsgate & Clacton

During July and August there will also be services to Walton and Felixstowe—see current handbills.

DAILY SERVICES (Excepting Fridays)
(Weather and other circumstances permitting.)

SOUTHEND, CLACTON.				SOUTHEND, MARGATE, RAMSGATE.		
	From 11th June *LAGUNA BELLE* on Suns., Mons. and Tues. only (except 13th and 27th June).	From 27th May *CRESTED EAGLE* or other Steamer.			From 19th June *GOLDEN EAGLE* or other Steamer (except 28th June).	From 27th May *ROYAL EAGLE* or other Steamer.
Pier.				Pier.		
TOWER	8.15 a.m.‡	8.40 a.m.†		TOWER	8.0 a.m.*	9.0 a.m.†
GREENWICH	8.45 ,,	9.10 ,,		GREENWICH	8.30 ,,	9.30 ,,
N. WOOLWICH	9.15 ,,	9.40 ,,		N. WOOLWICH	9.0 ,,	10.0 ,,
Gravesend	—	10.45 ,,		Tilbury	—	11.5 ,,
Southend	—	11.45 ,,		Southend	11.0 a.m.	12 noon
Clacton arr.	1.45 p.m.	1.45 p.m.		Margate	1.15 p.m.	2.0 p.m.
				Ramsgate arr.	—	2.45 ,,
				Ramsgate dep.	—	2.50 ,,
Clacton dep.	3.30 ,,	4.20 ,,		Margate	4.30 p.m.	3.45 ,,
Southend	—	6.20 ,,		Southend	6.30 ,,	5.45 ,,
Gravesend	—	7.15 ,,		TILBURY	—	6.45 ,,
N. WOOLWICH	7.50 p.m.	8.15 ,,		N. WOOLWICH	8.30 p.m.	7.45 ,,
GREENWICH	8.20 ,,	8.45 ,,		GREENWICH	9.0 ,,	8.15 ,,
TOWER	8.50 ,,	9.15 ,,		TOWER	9.30 ,,	8.45 ,,

* Sundays 15 minutes later.   † Saturdays 10 minutes later.   ‡ Sundays 10 minutes later.

FARES FROM LONDON
Children under 3 years of age free : under 14 half-price.

	"GOLDEN EAGLE"	"LAGUNA BELLE"	"CRESTED EAGLE"	"ROYAL EAGLE"
Day Return *Mon., Tues., Wed., Thurs.	SOUTHEND .. 3/- MARGATE .. 4/6	CLACTON .. 4/- Mon. & Tues. only	SOUTHEND .. 4/- CLACTON .. 6/-	SOUTHEND .. 4/- MARGATE .. 8/- RAMSGATE .. 9/-
Day Return, Saturday and Sunday	SOUTHEND .. 4/- MARGATE—Sat. 6/- ,, Sun. 8/-	CLACTON .. 5/- Sunday only	SOUTHEND .. 5/- CLACTON—Sat. 6/- ,, Sun. 8/-	SOUTHEND .. 5/- MARGATE .. 10/- RAMSGATE .. 11/-
Period Return	SOUTHEND .. 5/- MARGATE .. 9/-	CLACTON .. 9/-	SOUTHEND .. 5/- CLACTON .. 9/-	SOUTHEND .. 5/- MARGATE .. 10/- RAMSGATE .. 11/-
Single	SOUTHEND .. 3/- MARGATE .. 6/-	CLACTON .. 5/6	SOUTHEND .. 3/- CLACTON .. 5/6	SOUTHEND .. 3/- MARGATE .. 6/- RAMSGATE .. 6/6

Passengers are only carried on the Terms and Conditions printed on the Company's Tickets.
Day Passengers to Ramsgate do not land.
No Luggage allowed to Day-Trip Passengers.   * All Bank Holiday Day-Return fares at Saturday Day-Return Fares.
Supplementary charge for use of Sun Deck on "Royal Eagle" 1/- for the single journey, payable on board.

CIRCULAR RAIL & BOAT BOOKINGS from Tower, Greenwich or N. Woolwich Piers
Down by STEAMER, returning by RAIL, any train, 3rd Class.

To SOUTHEND, returning to Fenchurch Street by L.M.S. route or to Liverpool Street by L.N.E.R. route. Issued daily (except Fridays). Available during the season **5/-**

To MARGATE or RAMSGATE, returning by Southern Railway, any train, 3rd Class. Available for one calendar month **12/-**
Tickets also issued from Margate and Ramsgate to London Piers by Boat, returning by Rail.

To CLACTON, WALTON or FELIXSTOWE, returning by L.N.E.R. on any day within one calendar month, including date of issue **12/-**
Tickets also issued in the reverse direction, i.e. Rail from Liverpool Street to Clacton, returning by Boat on any day (except Fridays) within one calendar month, including date of issue.
Children under 14 half-fare.

Page Seventy-two

As the storm clouds developed over Europe, the General Steam Navigation Company published its timetable for 1939.

Four

The Declining Years: 1939-1999

In September 1939, the Thames paddle steamers were employed to transport evacuees from London to 'safe' resorts along the Essex and East-Anglian coast. Here the *Crested Eagle* disembarks children at Felixstowe, after a journey from Dagenham. This was to be the last occasion on which the *Crested Eagle* visited Felixstowe, as she was sunk during the evacuation from Dunkirk in May 1940.

The *Medway Queen* was fitted out at Deptford and commissioned as a minesweeper. She joined the 10th Minesweeping Flotilla and is seen here at Dover early in the war.

In May 1940 the *Medway Queen* was involved in the Dunkirk evacuation. She made seven journeys to the beaches and saved the lives of an estimated 7,000 soldiers. Constantly under attack, she is pictured here on what is reputed to be her first trip across the channel to the beaches of Dunkirk.

A Lewis gunner photographed aboard the *Medway Queen*. During the Dunkirk evacuation, it was with weapons such as this, and the guns obtained from rescued soldiers, that the vessel defended herself against constant air attack. While returning to Kent on 28 May 1940, the *Medway Queen* went to the aid of the striken paddle steamer *Brighton Belle* which was sinking near the North Goodwin Sands. She took aboard some 800 soldiers, the ship's crew and a dog!

The New Medway Steam Packet Company's steamer *City of Rochester* was not to survive the war. She was destroyed by bombing in 1940 and sank into the mud of the river that she had served for thirty-seven years.

A camouflaged *Royal Eagle* passes HMS *Whitehall* during the war. The date is unknown, but the location is probably the Thames estuary. The *Royal Eagle* served as an anti-aircraft vessel in the Thames Special Service Flotilla. She made three trips to the beaches of Dunkirk in 1940 and was one of the first allied vessels to enter Antwerp in November 1944.

The *Queen of Thanet* returned to the ranks of naval minesweepers in 1940. She was part of the 7th Minesweeping Flotilla based at Granton, Scotland, where this photograph was taken by a member of her wartime crew.

Some of the crew of *Medway Queen* photographed during minesweeping duties off Flamborough Head. They have since been identified and are recorded as follows. Left to right, seated: Robbie, Jim Day, Arthur Maraga, Jimmy James with 'Spot'. On the deck, left to right: Albert Nason, Bruce Sutton, Charlie Walker.

The *Medway Queen* led a charmed life and survived the war. She was refitted for excursion work at Thornycroft's Yard, Southampton, and returned to the Thames and her old haunts in 1947. She is seen here at Southampton on 2 March 1946 with the work well advanced.

The *Queen of Kent* had also served with the 7th Minesweeping Flotilla at Granton, under the command of Lieutenant Commander Dixon. She was refitted for excursion work at the Acorn Shipyard, Rochester, where this photograph was taken in 1946.

Of the old 'Belle Steamers' fleet, only the *Essex Queen* was considered to be worthy of post-war service. She was sold to new owners and left for Devon. Renamed *Pride of Devon*, she is seen here at Haldon Pier, Torquay, *c.*1947 She was eventually sold to Thomas Ward at Grays for scrap and returned to the Thames for the final time in March 1951.

The *Royal Eagle* returned to her usual Thames services in 1946 and is photographed here leaving Southend-on-Sea. The *Royal Eagle* remained in service until 1950 when she was withdrawn and laid up.

THE QUEEN OF THE CHANNEL, RAMSGATE.   D 15677

The General Steam Navigation Company had not only lost the *Crested Eagle* on war service, they had also lost the motor vessels *Queen of the Channel* and *Royal Sovereign*. To replace these they ordered two new ships from Denny's at Dumbarton. This is the second of those, the *Queen of the Channel*, which entered service in 1949.

The *Medway Queen* remained in service and appeared at the Coronation Review, Spithead, in June 1953.

The numbers of passengers carried to Kent during the late 1940s did not warrant the number of ships available. The older paddle steamers were vulnerable. Some were sold and left the Thames, while others were laid up. This is the *Royal Eagle* photographed at Whitewall Creek on the Medway during 1951. The *Golden Eagle* had already gone to the breakers earlier that year.

The General Steam Navigation Company was reported not to have wanted the *Royal Eagle* to be scrapped. However, there were no buyers and her deteriorating condition led to the inevitable. In 1953 she was towed from the Medway to the ship-breakers at Grays, where she is pictured with demolition well advanced.

The *Medway Queen* approaches Herne Bay pier in August 1957. By this date she was the last operational Thames excursion paddle steamer.

By 1960, with the exception of *Medway Queen*, the only paddle steamers to be found in regular use on the Thames, were the Woolwich Ferries. The *John Benn* had been built in 1930 and is seen here, *c.*1960.

The *Medway Queen* soldiered on into the new decade. She is seen here at Herne Bay in the summer of 1962.

In September 1963 the South Coast paddle steamer *Consul* was chartered for a few days and ran excursions along the Thames. This photograph was taken as she passed Tilbury, on one of her few trips before returning to Weymouth and an uncertain future. Built in 1896, the *Consul* was broken up at Southampton during 1968.

At the end of the 1963 season the *Medway Queen* was laid up and there was considerable speculation as to her future. She is pictured here in January 1965, on a rainy day at Rotherhithe, with her master, Captain Leonard Horsham. An inspection would soon decide *Medway Queen*'s fate.

The *Medway Queen* is seen here leaving Southend Pier on 31 August 1963. This was the last year the *Medway Queen* was operational.

The *Medway Queen* leaves the Thames under tow for the Isle of Wight, in September 1965. Her departure marked the end of an era. She was the last purpose-built Thames paddle steamer and her withdrawal was met with great sadness.

In 1965 an attempt was made to reintroduce paddle steamer excursions to the Thames. The Clyde paddle steamer *Jeanie Deans* was purchased and in November sailed to London, where she was fitted out at great cost. Renamed *Queen of the South*, she is seen here in Tilbury Basin, with the ill-fated motor vessel *Lochinvar*, soon after her arrival on the Thames, probably in January 1966.

During 1966 and 1967 the *Queen of the South* sailed from Tower Pier on a range of excursions to the Essex and Kent coasts. Sadly, her services lacked the success they deserved and this fine vessel departed for Belgian ship-breakers in December 1967. She is pictured here raising steam at Tower Pier, while behind, the motor vessel *Queen of the Channel* passes on one of her last trips to Kent, during the summer of 1966.

The demise of paddle steamers elsewhere in the country resulted in a number of the ships appearing on the Thames in static roles. The fine-looking Clyde paddle steamer *Caledonia* appeared as a restaurant and bar on the Embankment and was renamed *Old Caledonia*. This photograph was taken in 1974.

The fire-ravaged hulk of the *Old Caledonia*. Fire brought an untimely end to a popular Thames-side meeting place in April 1980. Found to be beyond economical repair, the *Old Caledonia* was towed away and broken up a few months later.

In 1971, the Dunkirk and veteran South Coast paddle steamer *Princess Elizabeth* was moored at Old Swan Pier as a restaurant and entertainment centre. She remained there until 1987 when she was sold to French interests and moved to Paris. She is seen here in September 1978.

The *Princess Elizabeth* photographed on the lower Thames, soon after being moved from her London moorings in 1987. The *Princess Elizabeth*'s final voyage to France, in December 1987, was interrupted by the weather and the towing vessel wisely put into Dover. The *Princess Elizabeth* had served at Dover with the *Medway Queen*, during 1940.

During September 1968, the Isle of Wight paddle steamer *Ryde* appeared on the Thames advertising 'Gilby's Gin'. The *Ryde* was fast approaching the end of her seagoing career and was soon sold by British Railways. She later replaced the *Medway Queen* on the Isle of Wight where she still remains. This photograph was taken while the *Ryde* was laid up in Portsmouth, *c*.1969.

The paddle steamer *Tattershall Castle*, built as a Humber ferry in 1934, still remains on the Thames Embankment as a restaurant and bar. Her engines are intact and she has been sympathetically converted to her new role.

The beautifully-restored river paddle steamer *Kingswear Castle*, built in 1926, is presently based on the River Medway, where she was photographed in 1986. Both she and the paddle steamer *Waverley* exist through the hard work and determination of their operating companies and the Paddle Steamer Preservation Society.

The *Waverley* is the last seagoing paddle steamer in the world. She is photographed here on the Medway, with the *Kingswear Castle*, during the summer of 1986. In the background is a forlorn and sunken, *Medway Queen*.

The *Waverley* is usually based on the Clyde. However, in recent years her annual visit to the Thames has given her passengers the chance to once again enjoy a Thames excursion. Here, Southend Pier is seen from the *Waverley* as she leaves on a trip to the Thames forts, on a blustery day the 9 October 1988.

On a few occasions during the last decade, the restored motor vessel *Balmoral* has provided the opportunity to experience again the long East Coast excursion from London to Great Yarmouth. The *Balmoral* is seen here leaving Lowestoft for London in 1996.

After returning to the Medway from the Isle of Wight on a semi-submersible barge in 1984, *Medway Queen* passed into the hands of the Medway Queen Preservation Society. The scale of the projected 'preservation' work can be seen clearly in this photograph.

The *Medway Queen*, afloat for the short trip to her new moorings at Kingsnorth, in November 1987.

The *Medway Queen* seen at her Kingsnorth moorings in July 1989. She has sunk once again, but the preservation work is well underway through the efforts of a team of dedicated volunteers.

The *Medway Queen*, the last remaining traditional Thames paddle steamer, a Dunkirk veteran and a part of our maritime heritage, appears resplendent at her moorings on the Hoo Peninsula in 1997. However, looks are deceptive and *Medway Queen*'s extremely frail structure threatens her very existence. At the time of writing her future is far from assured.

Acknowledgements

When compiling any book, I am acutely aware that there are many people who, over the years, have sent me photographs – often personal and valuable mementos of years gone past – which have added to my knowledge and ultimately to this book. To those thoughtful and trusting people I am very grateful. However, there are others whose efforts linked to this text have been extensive and I must mention the following, without whom this book would never have been completed: Rachel Baldwin (Walton Maritime Museum), Colin Tod (Felixstowe Museum at Languard Point), Noreen Chambers (Medway Queen Preservation Society), David Hodge (National Maritime Museum) Alex Duncan, Alistair Deayton, Winifred Box, Myra Allen, John Allen, Hugh Turner, William Prynne, Peter Stocker, Mike Dunn, Alison Paul, John Goss, Patricia Davenport, Tom Lee, A. Rees (ex-HMS *Queen of Thanet*), John Hart and Elisabeth Jones. All have given extensively of their time and knowledge. Lastly, special mention should be given to Peter Allard who, again, has allowed me to draw on his knowledge and photographic collection, to Andrew Gladwell (Paddle Steamer Preservation Society), who has helped so much with the collection of photographic material and to Miss Anne Barker who, following a chance meeting, has allowed us to see some of her late uncle, Sydney Renall's, unique Thames photographs.